JACK MUNDEY IN RED SQUARE

By the same author:

Rare Bird

JACK MUNDEY IN RED SQUARE

JAMES LUCAS

RECENT WORK PRESS
2015-2025
10 YEARS OF POETRY

Jack Mundey in Red Square
Recent Work Press
Canberra, Australia

Copyright © James Lucas, 2025

ISBN: 9781763670181 (paperback)

 A catalogue record for this book is available from the National Library of Australia

All rights reserved. This book is copyright. Except for private study, research, criticism or reviews as permitted under the Copyright Act, no part of this book may be reproduced, stored in a retrieval system, or transmitted in any form by any means without prior written permission. Enquiries should be addressed to the publisher.

Cover image: 'Minnamurra River- Courage Tree- initial sketch' by Drew Truslove, reproduced with permission of the artist.
Cover design: Recent Work Press
Set by Recent Work Press

recentworkpress.com
10 YEARS OF POETRY

For my parents

Contents

JAMES MARTIN AND JAMES MARTIN

Big Hug	3
Open the Frog App	4
The Incinerator Art Space	5
Architects	7
James Martin and James Martin	8

FERAL

Numbskull	15
Sunflowers	16
The Meat Olympics	17
Dodge the Dodo	18
Flea	20
Black Dog	21
Angophoras	22
Monstrous	24
Feral	26

RAIN

Last Call	33
Nothing to Declare	34
Turkey suburbiensis	35
Trip Advisor	36
a bento box	39
The Small Hours	44
Rain	45

DUET

RUOK?	53
Imagine	54
Jack Mundey in Red Square	55
Inheritance	57
Sightings	59
Riverwalk, Lane Cove	68
Sydney Modern	71
Mother and Child	72
Easter Weekend, Saint Kilda	75
Whaling	76
Not Looking for a Platypus	78
Duet	79
P.S.	84

If past, present and future are the dimensions of time, they are notoriously fluid.
Angela Carter, *The Infernal Desire Machines of Doctor Hoffman*.

JAMES MARTIN AND JAMES MARTIN

Big Hug

Hooked from behind into your sister's lap
you're grasped under both arms, fast held back
a sky-diver's arced up for tummy time,
toes pushing taut your terry-towelling suit,
the triple zero of your mouth and eyes
calling on silent: at your ear, breathing you know,
the same voice heard through the womb wall
meaning you're safe in maximum freefall.
When the earth's curvature flattens to prose
will you agree to stow Dad's nylon neat
before you walk from his collapsed conceit—
a tandem jump made on a single chute—
and wonder, did you leap or were you thrown
back when stone could be feather, feather stone?

Open the Frog App

Open the frog app. This is an app for collecting facts.
Record and upload. A singer's added to the frog song map.
The frog app is a translation app. I record clapsticks
and duelling washboards. I record a zydeco band.
Common eastern froglet is what the Australian Museum sends back.
Thank you for being part of our census. Why not join us on earbud safari?
The *green stream frog* shrugs its styrofoam package;
the *southern barred frog* shells peas in a box made of timber
the *striped marsh* is chopping; this fretsaw work is the *wallum rocket*;
the *broad-palmed frog* thumbs a comb nonchalant
as the *eastern banjo* who's floating up lobs.
I once asked, like a fool, where the tennis club was.
But with the frog app I found acceptance, found the guide
who leads me from avant garde throat singers, hiccupping buddhas,
back to the science of relative spawn depths, months for mating,
species distribution maps. Getting up close
the frog tells me whose pupils are vertical, round or flat
and bears unflinching witness to blemishes, spots and bands.
The frog app will not curate online personae.
Its expert identifications are cleansing a twittersphere
shouting alternative facts. For civil and well-informed discourse
open the frog app. Top up your swamp. Replenish the tank.

The Incinerator Art Space

Drawings by Drew Truslove, February 2024

Inside the shell by Burley Griffin,
held up by her protest
diet of coffee, meringue and lemon,

she's turning from work to work
to catch nine views in pen and ink
from one point straddling the creek:

Flat Rock Gully in the round.
'It's wonderful… just like… it's as if…'
She's standing tall as if illusions

of landscape can be metabolised
inside a furnace decommissioned,
its humming apparatus stripped.

The churning trash, all the ash
butterflies have settled or flown.
'It's just like… it's as if… this work

is very fine.' Calibrations of line
width and ultramarine blooms
lift boughs into the breaking light,

hold twig and leaf and sun and sap,
hold a memory surfacing
of stepping stones across quick water

and hold us still, hours later,
ablaze in that gully on the sunlit
side of the rust-locked steel door.

Architects

Oatlands, Tasmania

The high street measured out in Georgian stone
with cottages as well-proportioned as the manse
appears the work of just one architect
versed in the golden ratio. Symmetry of windows,
rooves without eaves: houses a child might draw,
a child with perfect pitch who knows how winter
can be made just bearable with double chimneys
in a midlands town raised in the child-like faith
that balanced form and decorative restraint
will breed gentility. Bootmaker, squire, comandante
pass through their homes' precisely centred doors
                            just as the curious eye enters
Arthur's Proclamation Board nailed to the five mile gum
via the centred handshake between the Governor
and what a Hobart draughtsman pictures as a 'chief',
their clasped hands holding by invisible thread
a line bisecting lower panels perfectly in balance:
x props his blooded spear, y his hot musket
up against the tree from which
                            in theory both are strung.
To complete this short course in geometry,
ask the draughtsman (not the child) to draw a line
east-west through Oatlands then rotate it
anti-clockwise ten degrees, translate it south and east.
                    Tomorrow they will clean the slate.
                    Tonight a pianoforte will play Bach.

James Martin and James Martin

*Matching statues of a young James Martin, for whom
Martin Place in Sydney is named, have stood in Parramatta
Square and Martin Place since 2022.*

He quits the stables cottage before dawn,
so quiet his drowsing mother's not disturbed,
James Martin, twelve, eldest son

of the chief steward and groom to Governor Bourke.
The Governor's blood horses snort and fret
in stalls where father, hard at work,

curry-combs a mare, Bourke's favourite.
James visualises thigh-thick stallion cock
as he speeds by the twin-dome silhouette

of the observatory weighing gems that fence the dark,
then passes by the Governor's great house.
Convicts built that. He's not of convict stock.

Down Domain Hill's wet grass his stride is loose
as he's attended by the bottle greens,
grain yellows and red necks, clear morning blues

of four Rose-Hillers, the same feathers he's seen
in possum skin hats of currency lads
he envies: he was born a year too soon

to be the son of the Australian soil
he longs to be. But he's no counterfeit.
He'll walk the thirteen miles to school.

The sun, not forgiving long-odds bets,
waits still below the twin towers of Saint John's,
seeps under pubs and barracks on George Street

and then erupts to blind the groggy town.
And so James fixes his eyes on the road.
He will walk thirteen miles into that sun,

wanting, perhaps, the shard of glass he smoked
over a candle to view the eclipse.
Bourke's blind to stars. Brisbane's telescope

took its pick. James needs just the Cyclops
stare he meets on Sydney Road. He checks,
composes a raised chin and compressed lips

as if this new day were a sculptor bent
on taking his impression as he stands
there by his motto: Either I will find

the way or make it. He's conned it in Latin
translation with his convict-master's aid:
Aut viam inveniam aut faciam.

He walks in workman's boots in that boy's stride
that skips enough to skirt round new-laid brick
and tread the dew or sandy verge that's kind

to marching feet, his satchel on his back
and, come to hand through a wrinkle in time,
in his right palm he holds an open book,

the Homer he'll receive as next year's prize.
He looks beyond the page to scan a yard
of steaming pigs for Circe cast in bronze.

Avoiding scattered dung, he listens sharp
for ringing horseshoes, duller bullock hooves
of the first carriage or first produce cart.

Son of the Governor's own groom,
known to town and gentry, he's no fool
to walk when with a smile and lifted thumb

he might ride a wagon of hay to school,
or sit beside this coachman on his box;
Sir John Jamison's groom with casual skill

slows to monkey grip young James aloft,
so while the boy of bronze walks thirteen miles
admonishing the roadway stooping south

avoiding marshes to straighten its spine,
the boy up on the box is free to dream,
relieved that he'll be writing no more lines

for a master emancipist and thief
and, thankful he has nothing to repent,
takes from his pocket a eucalypt leaf,

crushes it, inhales the menthol scent
just like his hero Mr Wentworth whose
brave speeches in the Sydney Gazette

are read by father in exultant voice.
Father says the towers of Saint John's,
the very walls of the Governor's house

are brick rendered then lined to pass for stone.
The new bridge at Duck River is half built.
Some miles ago road crews discarded irons.

Lollipop prop, a brunette in high vis
stands by a private road to promised land
where Macarthur scowls at his kippers and eggs.

They say New South Wales' richest man is mad.
Young James has hitched a ride that must outstrip
the legacies of rum money, blue blood

for improved minds and land, citizenship,
enterprise, bark and slab inns,
carriage repairers, pre-owned dealerships

in trucks and cars and light commercial vans.
At Haymarket the boy will disembark
to walk the last few blocks detailing plans

to copy last night's prep—sir's sure to check.
But it's too late for lessons. He's too late
to interview for journalist or clerk,

too late to Premier his fledgling state,
too late to make his way through glass-fired towers.
Greek chalkboard scrawl looks on a vacant seat.

In the plaza it's the sunset hour.
There's a line for pasta, salad, bread,
hierarchies of decline as the sun lowers

from unthinking gait to stiff-hipped step,
concern to unconcern about a collar,
white skin patched with sunburn, sparrow chest.

They queue now with good humour in good order
averting eyes or blinking as they look
into the sun, flanked by and rubbing shoulders

with a bronze boy holding an open book
innocuously marshalling the line,
the boy who's striding westward over a plaque:

raised in servant's quarters, Irish born,
this boy beat poverty, discrimination,
to become Chief Justice, Premier. The Hon.

Dom Perrottet unveiled this champion
of self-reliance, architect of public good
one hundred and ninety years after James Martin

(no mention here of fees and hitch-hiked rides)
first strode off to his Sydney school.
A public reprimand. Statues are tools.

FERAL

Numbskull

To build a wall me-high from fuel dropped loose
without care on the verge and to offset
each knuckle-knotted wedge for handy use
is easily earnt, easily spent sweat.
To divine seams where woodgrain wants to split
and Jenga-select apt chunks from the pile
and weave the kindling ready to be lit
puts no resolve or pleasure to the trial.
What I want is the bite of ironbark,
larrikin spikes that quill unseasoned flesh
then take an hour or day to work above
skin swollen, tenderised. This happy task
dispenses acupuncture to refresh
a dull and dulled man who will not wear gloves.

Sunflowers

up periscope.
bees vibrate

on tweeters, woofers.
fuzzed discs speak

beat sutras.
pupils swamp

gold irises
of sun seeking

mona lisas
with faraway eyes

like eclipsed suns
or flaming zeros

counted down
to sulphur crested

cockatoo apocalypse.
the shredding beaks.

The Meat Olympics

Paris 2024. This pavilion where a month ago
elite powerlifters clean and jerked
self-salted with ammonia.
                                        Zero odour:
flesh won't ripen in the trade hall
cooled to Fahrenheit 50 degrees.
We've just three hours to make chef-ready
side of pork, side of beef, five chickens
and a lamb, no fat, no bone, no tissue
gone to waste. No time to be pissed
at the tally-hyped gold-dazzled journo
who dubs this *the Meat Olympics*
(no muscle twitch here, fast or slow)
with his wank question: *is butchery an art?*
I'm no Michel-bloody-angelo
assessing marbling for a one-off cut,
I'm an expert in reduction of a carcase
to received forms of pragmatic anatomy.
Compulsory elements. Plus innovations that extend
flavour profiles and the bounds of cookability.
To feed. To nourish. Birds and beasts
lie on the block ungarnished by cloth,
fruit, or feathers, lit from inside
by myoglobin
                                        inhalation
as I bear witness to this demonstrable
transfiguration of the body, livid pork
suffusing to a peach and cream complexion
or grain-fed beef, blue-tinged, breathing in
Barossa red as on a steel scimitar it butterflies.

Dodge the Dodo

After Frank O'Hara

It's 10:15 on George a Tuesday
call it a rostered off day
I take slow admiring the art deco
lobby of the Dymocks Building
because somewhere up above is Birdland
who've rung to tell me my Esbjörn Svensson Trio
Good Morning Susie Soho has come in

and I'm sidling up to four Otis crates
out of the 1930s as sockless hipster execs
risk barked ankles from goods deliveries
and I even take the time to read
above the foyer clock *time conquers all*
which it told me Monday, when Birdland was closed

                              but today it's open
the cage labours four floors
more brush turkey than Charlie Parker
while I'm thinking all the shops I want
nest high in heritage building
corner suites
                    rucksack repairs, jazz CDs

I pick up the EST and flick desultorily
through sales table discs almost buying
an old Catholics (not on sale) then walk
four flights to daylight, the mall,
consider picking up some socks and jocks

but on a third thought drop into JB Hi Fi
on the chance they've YoYo Ma's Bach cello suites
(they don't) which I'm after as a gift

but it's OK I remember other music outlets
(classical music outlets) which I google
but there's nothing now Fish on George has closed
ditto Michael's Music Room
and that place in the QVB top gallery
I'm sweating by the time I get there
                              there's no sign of it
another eaterie, it's all high-end
accessories and landfill ready clothes
and of Yo Yo who sold out the Opera House
last week and whose spruce-speaking gut
upscaled our impulse likes and piques
to places outside grief and love
there is no trace; if he exists
it's as a string of ones and zeros
and he may or may not feel something
what exactly I'm not sure's been lost
maybe some way we had of breathing.

Flea

Sydney Olympic stadium, 4 February 2023

Mark but this Flea:
        his peppered shrinkwrap

wraps two bloods, sex
        -agenarian & brat punk,

two bloods slap bass pumps:
        blood old as gooney spoor

through shag, old as biceps
        flexing Hendrix,

old as skinned-in sweetmeats;
        & blood young as a bod

gym junked, young
        as the fifth limb funk

-monking licks to Cali
        -fornication; in the mix

a walking handstand
        the rim of the moshpit

balanced as long on the palette
        unsloshed sugar magik spunk.

Black Dog

It's a chore. And I'm tired. So an impatient child
siege engine all elbows and knees, and dog-eared
pages trip me down—what? A rabbit hole?
A canyon slot. Game without ladders. Just the snake
whipping to kink as a snagged rope flicked
feels the pull of the one way route. I'm blue despite
a neoprene suit. The gulch tightens. Figures are ghosts.
Stormwaters force through a close stone throat.
Choke it back. Breathe out slowly. Watch the chill rise.
Get a grip. Climb towards rumours of light.
Where I surface. Shucked wetsuit a zip and rip leech.
And I finger the dog's ear. All is quiet on the leash.
But a rope wanting coiling might yet snare the foot
of the child climbing into my lap with her book.

Angophoras

*

Belle of the B & S.
Cellulite dimples. Muscle.

*

Country girls
teach themselves
Balinese dance
wrist rotations.

*

Gymnasts of promise
ran off to join the circus.

*

Conté crayons
dust your fingers:
this is a doodle, not a
drawing.

*

Laughter cardiogram.
Catalogue of double joints.

*

High divers
breaking ground
in peach swimsuits.

*

Swiss Army implements
akimbo
to prise stodge from sprawl

*

Record attempts
for tricks with string.

*

Krumping for seniors.

Monstrous

He's gone. The man we think we know
is bled to nought. It's Act Three of the play.
His faith is shot. He asks himself: Why?

His age? His race? And we adjust
our understanding: taunts thrown in his face
do damage him. He's dirt to his fair wife

and he won't own what she detests, this wife
he is too green in love to see and know.
Her face is now as black as his own face

ugly with lust. But it's the ancient's play,
a ploy to drive men mad requiring just
our cultured intuitions. The question's why

the ancient seethes. We can't see why
he sweats on skinning boss and wife.
A routine workplace snub? Or is he just

plot function, not a mind that one could know,
Vice character who, in the mystery plays,
seduces Man? False friend with Janus face?

A sociopath? Far simpler. He too lost face
believing rumours of his wife. That's why
misogyny sours his every pithy play.

He deals a hand to silence any wife.
When her one hope is the car keys, he says no.
He's obliged to flout court orders. They're unjust.

Obiter dicta and the dissenting judge
blame women for imputed loss of face.
Proud fathers cut them off. No-one says no

to skirmishes in shaming, masked as wit. Why
humour this? Pity the naïve wife
who laughs it off as laddish banter, play,

comic relief. They don't do harmless play.
Those quibbles foolish, foul, and fair are just
three acts, an hour away from murdered wives.

Last act. The hero will not vandalise the face
he owns he loves. He weeps. He asks why
does heaven mock itself? Too late he knows

he is the pigeon in this play. And he can't face
what he calls love by a true name. He won't ask why
men kill their wives. But we know what we know.

Feral

1.

In the Gardens by the Yarra I run into Ferdinand Mueller
sowing, in the ashes of his billy fire, blackberry seed.
He looks like Friar Lawrence but fatter.
He's telling me there are no weeds. He knows his Shakespeare
just a little. That spells danger.
This is the Victorian era in which men know better.
You see the work of his hands prosper
in ditches and on both banks of the river
berries cluster thick as turds of thicket-panicked sheep.
Mueller's eyes see this, and further, his face ripened
to the purple of his portrait postage stamp,
his packet fat with decorations from the royal houses,
fat with the seed of *genus muellerina*. His lizard's longer
than a snake. His iridescent stag beetles
are matchbox muscle cars that shimmer lime and purple
glossier than boots shone sheepshit khaki.
He spills the billy, badgers me to find his statue,
rages at the Premier, rages against white-anting
Toorak aesthetes. We promenade, walk by the ponds,
while he makes plans for planting bluegum
into Africa and North and South America
and he assures me his work will continue in the pasture
science of acclimatised legumes and grasses, cattlefeed,
in hamburger patties by *Uber*. He's gone, not gone. I find myself
within this zoo for plants. And who am I to call him vandal?

2.

Voyages had their undersides,
wormy hulls hitch-hiked by shellfish,
ballast to the fox and rabbit

we'd decided would be coming to this country
in the circumstances we'd decided:
submariners, illegal immigrants and pioneers,

fore-runners to disgorgees
arriving by the harbourful when giant tankers purged
to ingest minerals that sweetened account deficits;

fore-runners to the giant wakame
mermaid tails who ate their mermaids,
to dinoflagellates who poisoned oysters.

Tim Low, walking on the shores
of D'Entrecasteaux Channel,
prised his last oyster from the rocks

and took in a free side of algae
courtesy of ballast from Japan.
You can read this in Low's *Feral Future*.

He'll point you to Port Philip Bay,
to seaworms thick under the hulls
as windsock carp at a kite festival

afloat on dusk. Night falls as a blanket
on the comatose, a loose weave
of seastars yellow as congealing deep-fry.

3.

I'm not fox. Call me ningani.
I who was fox, I have crossed
through many nations,
through Eora and through Dharug.
I crossed into Wiradjuri.
I ate lamb warm from the womb.
I have tasted bettong, bilby
(sent offshore for their protection).
I have felt the willy willy
sand the tongue of Karengappa.
Roadkill fed me
through Wangkangurru to Arrernte.
I've survived on litter bins.
I've dodged guns. Snubbed 1080.
Say ningani. Puwutjuma.
Show respect. I have my song.

4.

He curates fauna the most primitive on earth:
foolish marsupials, mere foetuses at birth,

grubs wriggling to their pseudo-wombs.
His copperplate puts a brave face

on ecological cringe: *animals of this class
must go down before invaders*

so far ahead in Darwinian terms
(Albert Le Souef, Taronga Park, 1923).

But inferiority's complex. Trees and shrubs
evolved on the eroded continent

promoted by aid agencies
lay claim to foreign lands farmed bare.

Wattle, silky oak, the casuarina's
fistfuls of nine inch nails

move in where vanished Africans
will never be repatriated.

Our wattles are exhausting
Cape Town's water with their thirst.

Expat melaleucas drink Miami swamps,
their shaggy manuscript rewriting highways.

5.

The host dies; the gene endures. The product's obsolescence
is the trademark's strength, no time lost in the brief flutter
from C.A.D. to landfill wherein desires propogate
geometrically in endless Next Gens. Economies of scale
secure full penetration of the market garden habitat.
Local species go the way of corner stores;
niche retailers seek shiftwork in the same malls
where young acquire their must-have strains of affluenza.
Like mall rat casuals sugar gliding on cheap calories
our natives learn to live with, then rely on pests.
As far as the eye can't see, the heart won't grieve.
Delete your documentaries. Focus on the new nature.
Wear fast fashion. Look to thickets of lantana
for bandicoots and whipbirds, fairywrens and scrubwrens,
Richmond birdwing butterflies, insects colonising carcasses,
reed bees nesting in the stems. Believe that paperbark apologists
find raccoon road-kill, woodpeckers among their trees.
Take solace in the eucalypts that feed African cooking fires.
Do what you must. See what you will.
Ningani in the August heat takes cover in the blackberry.

RAIN

Last Call

The regent honeyeater's song
is regent honeyeater wrong
but passable as wattlebird.
He had to copy what he heard

having no mentor of his kind
to seed true language in his mind,
the melody unheard or stilled:
air untuned to toneless wind.

A listening female hasn't met
a regent honeyeater yet.
In barren woods she might hear fall
a wattlebird's unwelcome call.

Dawn is her golden-tipped black wing.
She listens but she does not sing,
unmated, muted, deceived elf,
doomed bird who cannot sing herself.

Nothing to Declare

To hear the raptor speak
with human voice
its head must be freed
from the hood
its trussed wings freed
from the plastic
bottle in the footy sock

and only then and only if
you're one of the lucky ones
it's doped but not
asphyxiated it says
now the case is popped
all that it picked up inflight:
I hold creation in my foot.

A roost.
A roost in a clean cage.

Turkey suburbiensis

Dork descending. Snorting tenor sax
sounds from the birdman rally

on the roof. Feathers plummet
like tossed mulch, closing off a loop

to set my watch by: nature strip to
scat-stained steps to dog-defying

height of the dividing fence,
cavort through new shoots

honking bottom notes like Stan Getz,
back lawn promenade, ascent

to roof ridge. Launch. Compost
hits the street strutting honkytonk

to thrust a thermometer beak
in mounds toasty as slagheaps

where the boomtown chicks
hatch fledged and born to rort,

the way the bloke without charisma
who isn't even caskplonk

drunk trampling the flowerbeds
and is always last to leave the sharehouse

party somehow ends up with the lease.

Trip Advisor

Lockdown September 2021

First pick a gap. Approach the wall
of fridges and be patient with a man

interrogating yoghurt best before dates.
Be patient with a blue cheese crowd

who clot the flow through aisles
with no more elbow room

than cruise ships corridors.
Step on, unsteady as a reveller

on listing decks, an Irish dancer
not trusting her hands

who grips her trolley like a sea-rail
to survey the humming blue

expanse of product unavailable.
Refuse to be a buccaneer, raft up

to the Dunkirk flotilla. Be mindful
the masked man taking possession

of his tissues is no enemy,
that we learn by breaking habits.

Knead, tonight, a less generic flour,
try a basket of new brands

and then dream of South America,
of a dishevelled pilot smoking

on the Buenos Aires tarmac
three hours before touching us down

sideways in a Patagonian crosswind,
dream of a root-bound site where

we'll make camp between Glacier Gray
and the refugio, resist the pitch

of uneven ground as if on the inside
of a gyroscope. Secure in a down bag

dream that you jog a postcode
perimeter under a sky blank

with writer's block, dream inside
your personal space radius that touches

closed circumferences of trust
in a pocket, double-bagged, of civic life.

It's all OK. We'll start awake, unzip,
taste blown moraine coating the gums,

haul gear to the El Calafate
bus stand where you'll ask me

if I've got the tickets that we bought
with our bad Spanish though it's hard

to hear you when the wind
has not stopped coming off the water

through these many days and nights
in which I see a sorbent snout,

a wall of chilled milk, calving.

a   bento   box

1.

flight	in	3	days	airport		shuttle
hard	not	to	take	loop	the	looproads
as	hand		baggage	f	u j i	over
to			haneda	the	wrong	shoulder
japan			airlines			
runway			fireball			

in their 60s
in blue tunics
parking lot men
point orange wands

easy   signage
kanji   english
h i r a g a n a

the   light   switches
depress left   right

laundry   on   shirt
width   balconies

press   of   bodies
women   only
c a r r i a g e s
a   few   lost   men

ramen   with   miles
brubeck   sashimi
starbucks   satchmo
billie   fried chicken

tickets   to   ride
tickets   to   eat

one   room   wide
hotel   swaying
with   my   deaf   ear
s i n u s i t i s

feel   a   tremor?
set   doors   ajar
to   safeguard   exit

2.

dearest   apples
of   nagano
full   swollen   fruit
of   trees   pruned   squat

branches   thinned
for   even   sun
around   the   base
reflective   foil

tans   evenly
every   crisp   globe
juice   jupiters
eclipse   the   palm

dearest   apples
of   nagano
red   planets   set
on   display   tables

7   Eleven
too   much   butter
too   much   mayo

paul   grabowski
says   the   waiter

hung   on   the   street
cedar   twig   balls
turn   green   to   brown
as   sake   mellows

suburban   kerb
vending   machines

formal   culture
of   gift   giving
sustains   quarter
acre   orchards

11   seats   *leave*
it   *to*   *me* the
only   english
on   the   menu

plum   wine   on   ice
fresh   w   a   s   a   b   i

japanese   or
western   breakfast
eat   your   poached   egg
using   chopsticks

3.

sheathed   in   bamboo
immune   to   flame
the   wooden   pole
by   which   a   pot's
hung   over   fire

spears   a   wood   fish
the   second   guard
a   water   symbol

above   all   an
i r r e g u l a r
h o r i z o n t a l
wooden   lattice
in   which   smaller
a p e r t u r e s
draw   all   the   smoke
thru   the   large   hole

paper   cranes
in   rainbow   garlands

white   plaster   walls
streaks   of   black   rain

melted   buddhas
workers   bleeding
from   their   tongues

the   injured   drink
black   rain   the   rain

a   day   excursion
by   shinkansen

horses   tapped   for
blood   transfusions

age   three   riding
a   tricycle
he   died   groaning
water   water

4.

overnight snow
steep roof easels
of blank paper

boots skis skiers
c o u r t e s y bus
c o n t o r t i o n i s t s
whatever numb
er double it

overnight snow
c a l l i g r a p h y
of fewer strokes

chairlift pylons
loudspeak coltrane's
favourite things

golyu means 4
dragons shinto
p r a c t i t i o n e r s
will not climb peaks

towies wirebrush
snow from chairs
reach for the bar
grab only air

overnight snow
tips dorsal fin

white horse grazing
is the snowmelt:
time to plough fields
in h a k u b a

shared gondola
czech bagpiper
touring folk punk
ski instructor

adrift knee deep
sumos flounder
in underpants
j a n 2 6

5.

whistling arrow
shrills to battle

nine compartments
gourmet bento
k y o t o – t o k y o
s h i n k a n s e n

the window frames
a ribbon in
a h u r r i c a n e

no apartment
pets instead pet
café puppies pigs

yard wide gardens
for cloud pruning

in modest dress
enter on knees
avoid strong scent
a p p r e c i a t e
seasonal blooms
the chosen scroll
inspect the bowl
then place the bowl
on your left palm
turn it clockwise
9 0 d e g r e e s

the old man nods
over a thermos

o m o t e s a n d o
fashion houses
outside the square
a r c h i t e c t u r e
blow torch honey
comb and icebergs

girl metal band
head bang in sync
their ad on mute

in the train carriage

turn your phone off
keep your voice down

14 h u n d r e d
p a c i f y i n g
precious objects
buried beneath
the great temple

the manual of
d i s a p p e a r a n c e
in plain sight
vanished people
pay in cash
assume a name

The Small Hours

Half woken, hour unknown, I try to sort
the first notes of dawn chorus, airbrake wheeze,
from tawny frogmouth, motorbike that snorts

and Bon Scott shrills a free bitumen ecstacy
while all the while the dull fuzz of the clock
display's unreadable—insufferable tease.

A hand might spider to my glasses, and I'd sneak a look
if not that clock knowledge would too much rouse
the drowsy muscles wanting just to rock

here on the point of tipping back to sleep for hours.
The rub? To sleep is to invite the brute alarm
to trip my fly personae to the floor,

depopulate the dream's *nouveau romain*
with tyranny of just one conscious self
flicking the switch to sew my shadow on.

Rain

1.

Rain knuckles the roof off sync as Kitty Flanagan's idea
of jazz—*come on fellas, play together or don't play at all*—
then finds consensus, builds to an ovation, Beatlemania

and your own disquiet in even innocent hysteria's
proximity proves prescient in gutters
overwhelmed. See where toddlers painted outside walls

with dirt, snails at eye level? Rain's in the paperback that curls
up in your lap, in corrugated weekend papers,
rubber crackers. When sun-showers re-saturate

come in behind this bright curtain of beads before
it's blown to TV noise, before the evening stews, before
the front hits like a goon in pinstripes and the roof applauds.

2.

Under your feet the lawn gives like an unsprung mattress
like forgetful memory foam like spearmint sponge.
You daren't stand still: your feet settle unevenly

to cast doubt on foundations / hangover your balance.
Another gum loses its grip to menace postie bikes
that fishtail, buck, plough nature strip to paddock.

Stayers firm with bookies, toads in jacuzzis
ask no questions. Your feet squeegeeing grass
subside into the Winton Age of Dinosaurs Museum footage

of *australovenator* (call me Banjo) bogging
in a waterhole turned sink beyond her tip point
in an educational cartoon about what we knew and when. `

3.

What comes down must go up. The dam raises a dull face,
the pool its glass. The rain gauge spills its flute
of corked champagne. In creek lines, leaves and bark

and fallen limbs are treeforked like punk cubbies.
Concave bridges float toy cars. Drains geyser.
Curbs are leapt. Water doorknocks up the street

to hustle its case against common sense
or loiters at your back steps with malicious patience.
News crews discover inland seas with currents

of raw sewage, mosquito fog, main street archipelagos.
Angels gather up the faithful via helicopter winch
while inside a shrinking roof space batts ascend.

4.

The tempest stomps and drums, whistles and jeers: Miles Davis'
Bitches Brew scat sung by Ariel and Sycorax
until a backing vocal whine resolves into the outboard

of a neighbour's tinny. But he won't leave. He's proud
of having endured, of outlasting the bank,
the local branch at least. The magic's a delusion—

Ceres's wheat crop is ruined, Iris's bright silks are mothed,
the trees in whose knots spirits were locked
were cleared by chain—this occupancy too will pass,

an old man's howled command for the rain to stop
will pass. His island shrinks to comic strip proportions
and drowned books. Loosed Ariel, prising free loosed tiles, laughs.

5.

These skies like grey thoughts smudged by cheap eraser
lower over poem unwritten, unsent text,
a letterbox for ill-timed confidence,

ruined correspondence. Among the grey-scale myths
I see a white Shem who walks a black dog
rain-bombed by bipolar Tiddalik.

Tropes mobilise. Tropical parallels of latitude
slip like fatiguing hula hoops while the courageous
sandbag to defend the uninsurable, wire-brushing off

rank mould's buzzcut khaki. Poppies on the rain radar
bloom yellow, orange, crimson. The woodfire burner,
fixing a smoked eye on one more bunkered day, is king.

6.

A getaway. The far south coast. Surf broadcasts
what was, is, will be; thunder mimics surf but louder,
bully loud, while Jared Diamond warns gated communities

are fire and flood accelerants; the podcast is drowned out
as frogs under this house on stilts pull-start
the two-stroke that inflates its skirt of wraparound deck

and we're adrift. The shoreline recedes through the rain.
The engine throbs. Froglets raise mutinous heads
between warped boards. A dolphin torch drills like a chain

but finds no anchor point where the swamped fizzle,
slipping off the beam. Time to pretend
we're all aboard. Sing, *after me the rain*. Sing after me, *the rain*.

DUET

RUOK?

My question to tell if you are OK
in full knowledge that *yes* may well mean *no*
—monosyllables build the barricade
perimeter beyond which we can't go
into the sanctum where you admit fright,
a precious hell guarded from special op
humanitarian fact-finding flights—
must voice loving concern. And must stop
to wait on answers truly indirect,
accept teenager-brokered terms of love
are spoken in non-sequiturs and gaps,
a small concession I did not expect
enough to give stalled confidence a shove.
To tell us that you are OK perhaps.

Imagine

John Lennon climbs a ladder up to YES.
He peers through Yoko's magnifying glass,
the tiny smudge grows sharp, a word to bless
all that has passed and that will come to pass.

To peer through Yoko's magnifying glass
(each rung makes audible his rubber soul)
he leaves his past, grabs what will come to pass.
One word erases good-bye for hello.

No auditors check whispers in the soul.
Avant garde ladders have no foot for bills.
One word erases good-bye for hello.
He signs on with the fool upon the hill.

An iconoclast (for this he'll pay the bill)
reads one word on the ceiling, word to bless
himself, Yoko, and the fool on the hill.
John Lennon climbs the ladder up to YES.

Jack Mundey in Red Square

Tea and cake with a Trade Unionist is strange.
They've put him on the front veranda
of the hedge-blind house in Prince Edward Parade
for elevenses with the Kelly's Bush Battlers.
They see his broad paw snuff the sun
from bone china and the President wonders
if Mr Mundey might not prefer a more manly mug.
She's too well-bred to air the suggestion.
His nose is off straight. He's a thick head
of hair, he's at ease in his tangerine open-neck
shirt, brown off-the-rack jacket. A chewed-ear bear.
He's articulate. Tamed. Askin had smirked
at their 'Boil the Billy' media days. How Jack laughs
when told a conservative wag has dubbed
Prince Edward Parade, 'Red Square!'
They're chuffed. And he's charmed
by these morning-tea ladies raised on Menzies
to serve and safeguard Ming dynasty heirs,
the CBD husbands nonplussed
—then disgusted—with their bloody meddling.
How could they, blue-chip-kept women,
see past the Parade's median parkland
modelled, perhaps, on a Home Counties green,
to champion bracken fern, blueberry ash,
for sixty years spared from Kelly's furnace
—just regular scrub—from all he's seen?
Ex metal worker, Jack knows a bit
about smelters and toxins: unpleasantries
best kept to himself. What's wanted here

is strategy. How to gain ground from
how Jennings responds to this first 'Green Ban'?
Good coinage that: less abrasive than 'black'.
Adroit with tea service, he's the good sense
and tact not to say 'scab labour.'
He's arrangements to savour. This cup without sugar.

Inheritance

My grandfather's chairs have been delayed
by assiduous authorities,
run over by their sniffer dogs, x-rayed,
poor stiff-limbed mules, for secret cavities.

'Why would you choose to pay the freight
three times the cost of what you say they're worth
according to your import duty paid?'
Sentimental value. Before my birth

our family relocated overseas.
I met him twice. The second time
he was tall corner and rug-covered knees.
A voice and hands spoke in a thread of light

to ask, 'How many apples make a pair?'
I fill his fingers' open bowl with fruit,
weigh up imagined apples against pears
and hazard 'Three'. Words play me. Nous is mute.

You'd call this unfair riddle, playful trick.
I choose to think instead he itched to know
the way his grandson's mind was wired to tick.
He spiked my speech before he let me go

with 'misapprehension', 'idiosyncrasy'
but when the phone call told us he was dead
I didn't speak. True words eluded me.
Words short as grief. Words short as love and dread.

And forty years on, here's a wooden chair.
The front legs are corkscrewed like candycane.
Too much relief: we like lines clean and spare.
No corner of the house offers it space.

But I respect the craftsmanship, the frame
of good proportions, a strong form
pursued not to perpetuate a name
but to make well-enough to be hard-worn

a chair of lathe-turned, chisel-jointed oak,
imperfect making of a patient hand,
and I'm thinking again of words he spoke,
the distant corner where a small boy stands.

He asks, 'How many apples make a pair?'
I answer 'Three', and sit in this, his chair.

Sightings

Fields, of course, are made. Edward W Said

1.

Your chart's much-admired fidelity is to a shoreline
sketched in the ship's wake, an absolute
you have to imagine and then seize.
Across each bight and reach

your keel would cut and stitch a continent.
Circumnavigator, for all your expertise you're kin
to Tolstoy's peasant, setting out at dawn
to walk in his allotted day the boundaries of as big a field

as he can claim who's swallowed by the endless steppes.
Glass to your eye, you stand at the masthead
adding angles to a geometric sequence,
never looking down on scrolling marble:

your ideal is naming nothing for yourself,
indefatigable attention to the well-done task,
the good health of your men. While you make possible
sojourns ashore for scientific gentlemen, you've more respect

for Bongaree who you send stripped, brave fellow,
to make contact with each Indian band,
these *Australians* as you name them once or twice
in a gesture magnanimous as romantic

to a whitefella deaf to the unknown unknowns.
Some day when you run on a sandbank like a mine
tailing and ride the snake down to Mauritius,
to seven years exile, with Trim lost to some stomach

anonymous and hungry, you'll find monastic solace
in perfecting these charts for accuracy's sake,
your errant mind patrolling this lost coast
unsleeping as an AUKUS sub or a great white.

2.

Upturned Guinness that will not spill, white socked Trim,
midnight writing shore-break as your signature
with starlight on your breast, an underlip of beer froth,
why did they name you for a part in *Tristram Shandy*?

Sterne's shaggy puppy dog, sonar deaf, is floating
in a womb still as a billabong, an amniotic bath
erasing due dates, mocking clocks
on which seamen rely. No longitude without kept time.

Did your naming nod to the absurd as staff of life?
Your heart Trim is beating chrono-chaos
with moggie pizazz, persuading all the ships' chronometers
to purr freelance, steal a second here, proudly present

it there by a long tail of unaccounted consequence.
You jump cat on the map, the map slips off the table,
legs at 85 degrees to the horizon as if a pendulum,
held still, could break the past from quarantine:

when your right forefoot (carefully) then hind
steps down you're slipping off the rail to your baptism,
your sea burial—twice a kitten, you might drown
unless you swim and scale a rope and draw

a second rescue breath and listen to the weird
tides swimming in your swimmer's ear; or else
you feel yourself ossify into the sculpted pose
of your immortal self, propped against your old mate

as he squats in the throng of Euston Station, or his shadow
in the New South Wales State Library window,
or at Port Lincoln, threatening his sextant calculation,
set to trip him and the world to spin from in between his legs.

3.

Paddling air, split oars and chewed plank ends
hold their position, buoyish in the surf,
dispelling the illusion of a wreck. They're seals.
The sealers are long gone. Or not yet here.

Flippers, tails, a whiskered head dog-deep.
Were this a wreck she would have been a whaler
of eight oars and as many heavy wooden clubs
dispatched to seek out drinking water or to kill

fresh stores of meat. Here barrel flanks of seals
smooth the wash the way Brett Whiteley
flattens a broad brush not breaking
his stroke in wild seas of ink. Do not mistake

this flipper raised for a salute: blood
at the skin surface kisses cooling air
so shedding heat from fur-swathed casks of fat.
The sun goes and they drift in loose formation

to a drenched rock fringed by shaggy weed,
rasta Medusa guarding a secure pontoon,
rowdy terraces awash with seals who clamber
leech-fat, who usurp and interlope, teeth bared

or yawning. I've the luxury of speculation,
have the choice of leaner meat, no need of oil
to feed a hungry lamp. A tanker like a blue sky
prospectus for a geodesic survey passes

down the coast where you beat up into the gale,
the final leg, Mount Dromedary S30°W,
while dysentery carries off another seaman,
Thomas Smith. And only then the wind shifts.

4.

Throw a fish head on salt meat to bring up maggots.
Look for the fish head that stays clean.
Recall feasts of seal and mutton bird.
Kanguroo stewed by the hundredweight.

See the Gulf of Carpentaria's blue mud,
the stunted growth. Hear the ship's timbers.
Look up at the termite mounds.
Hear the ship's timbers croak. Hear carpenters report

Investigator, tight and sound, has barely a sound plank.
Wait out the monsoon season.
Cut back the lemon ration.
Hold this ship together by your force of will.

Throw a fish head on salt meat to bring up maggots.
Let the log record an Indian shot dead.
Look for the fish head that stays clean.
Hold this ship together by your force of will.

Put into Coepang for fresh buffalo and kid.
Buy up the suspect vegetables.
Cut back the lemon ration.
Look for the fish head that stays clean.

Dress opening wounds, ignore hallucinations.
Kanguroo and mutton bird and seal.
Stay calm when islands lie about their names.
Hold this ship together by your force of will.

Rub Trim's coat of friable crystal.
Pay your respects when Greenhalgh solves
the riddle: how much land does a man need?
Just the six feet he doesn't get at sea.

5.

London turns up lodgings like loose change: cheap,
cheaper again. You're seventy at forty and the Royal Navy's
skimping on your pension. In the colonies are raised,
along with statues, subscriptions for your widow Ann,

and Ann your child. One hundred years on Scott names you
discoverer of all the southern coast and never mind
the accidental details. And he's only thinking of the French.
Nausea has its specific interval: a pulse that's just

so many seconds as will drop me to my knees
should I pass in this light craft beyond the plunging Heads,
look back as an outsider. Better I had fixed on the horizon.
These days your uniform makes you an easy target.

The best that I can do is read your journals, also Scott,
Tim Flannery, and Jaya Savige, try to salvage
scuttled ships, frustrated by the silences of books
and Google's prompt irrelevancies, always knowing less

than an imagined figure loitering, chisel in pocket,
wanting after-hours access to the Library Foyer Map
as if it were correctible, the mosaic
of chipped rock, russet marble, of enemy-alien labour

furloughed from internment camps, accurate
to the west but its Cape York peninsular a dealership
tube man collapsed, the whole right flank
a blown-out dream of brief and insecure tenure.

Riverwalk, Lane Cove

Sun after the storm.
Skinks rising through the boardwalk.
Bubbles through boot seams.

*

Bellbirds: pitched above
kookaburra mania,
electronic pips.

*

A water dragon
stares down interruption.
Holds its yoga pose.

*

Fairyland pleasure
grounds under waist high weeds.
No ghosts. Just the sign.

*

A flash of blue wren:
busyness
too quick for the eye.

*

Flash-flood wheelie bins
lodged in mangroves
red lids flipped.

*

A low-down rumour:
a lizard's invisible
transit through litter.

*

Enamel parrots
unpick in flight
loose knots of angophora.

*

Pools on rock. Debris
of insects dead and living.
Fat tadpoles.

*

Mach one rosellas
point and wingman
rock their tips.

*

Echidna freezes:
punctured by 9-inch nails
this lung breathes.

*

From scribble to flightpath:
wren, mynah,
eastern osprey, phoebus.

*

A tawny frogmouth
turns a blind knot,
ruffles its splinters.

Sydney Modern

Shake up the guest list. I want intimate. I want A-list.
Scratch the Bracks. We'll do without their jaundiced
thin-lipped condescension. Ditto the Tuckers
their politicking grates. Can all the Melburnians.

The Blackmans have an aggrieved look, the Dickersons
a coconut milk junkie tinge. Desiccated Drysdales
amuse when riding the Nolans—'Ned my arse! Can't
sit a horse!'—but my god their uprooted root-crop wives

would turn you off your canapes. We'll have no red dust
on this polished concrete no Gleasons upsetting vegans
no Boyds gawping witless at the skylights. Cossington-Smiths
always arrive sunshower damp we'll do without their rainbow.

Keep the Prestons, though, they always send apologies, flowers
easily binned. Scrub the Cassabs who will front up unironed
from dossing down in Frank Gehry's brown paper bag.
The Dobells look like something out of Dickens. No thanks.

And the Longs and Bunnys would be bothering the Whiteleys
for spliffs and *they* always leave the door ajar on their two-backed
menagerie—posers, exhibitionists—likewise the Smarts
who attention-seek us to a detail to flaunt their celebrity.

So scratch the lot. Bring me the textile artist to the Emperor
of Ice Cream bring me the Minister for Party Lights bring me critics
for our restaurant-bar-cafès, financiers, and all who love
cleared cubic acres. Sliced bread gets more expensive every day.

Mother and Child

1.

You quicken. Tumble. You jab at the womb.
Push through the birth canal into the light.
You sit. And crawl. Stand tall to stumble walk.
From intent, lips and tongue, you forge a word.
You ask what only innocence could ask.
Milestones to mark. And learning verse
from Granny's Jack and Jill and curds and whey.
Your playmate passing on the common way,
she meets all the same milestones in reverse:
framing the question a toddler might ask,
her tongue tips to a word, meets mind the gap
on a ghost platform. Head inclined to walk,
she seeks an exit sign while there is light.
Someone tells her again: this is your home.

2.

Ferns spill from baskets slung beneath the roof.
Vines arm-wrestle the beams and eaves.
But are they real? A waiter works the proof,
threads through the tables culling yellowed leaves
from floor-level specimens. Do fakes fool
us, out of reach? She speaks of her friend
who says *every plant is plastic—even grass!*
We study our hot chocolates and friands.
*She spoke three languages. Can't read a book.
Extraordinary!* On the homebound drive she looks
in wonder on brick homes. All the white cars.
My eldest tells next year she's starting school.
Mum's drinking in our news, quick to forgive
all counterfeits swapped in for things that live.

3.

And she can laugh. She does laugh at herself.
My legs are alright. Pity about my head.
Connoisseur of the human comedy,
she loves her grandchild setting straight her son,
loves a boss toddler's swing set tyranny.
Topical jokes elude her. So do puns.
Acquired wisdom and the intelligent self
don't have a lot to work with: data shed,
her thoughts don't have the contexts that allow
a woman to negotiate the world.
As every hard-won freedom is reversed
options reduce, dilemmas multiply
and every task's a puzzle simplified
for pieces missing. Oldest player first.

Easter Weekend, Saint Kilda

Deathwish bar and tattoo parlour personnel in their themed tees
stand shopfront to review an El Camino Chevrolet
and brace of Hogs. The deep end of Acland Street.
You see a skateboard matador who turns a V8 off loose jeans,
you pass the sign for tarot and an impromptu boxing clinic,
pass Italians, fish n chips and four éclair shops, *Readings*
booksellers impasto gelato smear and palette knife
scrapings of dog, walk on past ghosts of genuflecting seniors
whose spook bowls indulge their biases on grown-over greens
where co-op veggie beds are raising ropey sunflowers
and scrap metal whimsy to keep out rough sleepers,
coming at last to Luna Park's impassable tramline knot,
the giant mouth Edvard Munching dental tools awhirr.
Look through the rollercoaster formwork to the pink sun
setting on a fake west coast. A number 16 tram departs
like a spat pill while patron Saint Paul looks on from his mural
on the Espy, harmonising guilt-cred with nostalgia for 13
hours on a bus, the Cross, this promenade both he and I prefer.

Whaling

Below the hull (we hope) are whales,
    below the planks, the roll motion
        sick who didn't take their pills,
on deck, those who watch east to dusk
    or squint west across blushered cheek
        –bone swell into a late sun nailed
like a doubloon in easy reach.
    We sail the cusp where light meets dark
        within a Caravaggio
of shadow sea, of sea sun-lamped.

    A cry goes up: flukes far ahead.
Our engine kicks and labours long
    as the held breath in which a whale sounds
        but nothing until aft, a spout;
the four points of the spotter's clock
    with bow at twelve, starboard at three
        (child's play within the harbour mouth)
wheel us through timezones and dates
    as on our right two forms as one
        slow blink of glass surface and wheel.

Whalechasers, satiated, cheer
    for innocence—not the whales', ours—
        something we had thought lost or maimed
has crowned though the caul and clot
    lights on an ocean wide enough
        to clean birth's bloody aftermath

and had I not six minutes' dive
        to think too hard about sincere
                noise as atonement insufficient
to the sanctioned crimes in which
        I know I play a role for which
                I'll never be arraigned, I'd feel
as the lighthouse dissolves
        into a measured pulse and we
                admit we're spotting blind as we
re-enter the dark anchorage
        past hidden Chowder Bay, I'd feel
                for one night everything is changed.

Not Looking for a Platypus

I saw a rock
slew weirdly

up the rapids'
stop start

gravity reversed
& I saw moss

ball on a log
drop & dissolve

& when at last
I saw the duck

-bill sweeping
gravel, oscillating

beaver tail
& visualised

its venomed feet
I had no witness

to this stumble
across wonder

not to be
dismissed as hoax.

Duet

ABC radio Classic FM, 11 November 2021

1. Improvisation

To find my way home I must listen
advises William Barton,
Tamara Anna Cislowska's guest.
It could be just the wind picking up leaves.

I hear the radio. I hear the rain
slap-dashing Morse across the glass
that dampens horns and mutes the trill
loosing drenched pedestrians

shot in a flash photograph.
Percussion shakes the City Circle.
I find a channel lane changing
past kayak-quiet bicycle and

indigestive bus my tyres
sashay across the Cahill
onto the through-arch Bridge
and high on this the third of eight

steel strings that thrum
I drive between steel colonnades
the long octaves of tuning forks
that stand tall asking to be struck.

2. Ave Maria

There are songlines through a war crime zone
and songlines through the open cut.

For dug-up smeltered lives we've songs
silenced like emptied village squares,

silenced like left behind mothers' tongues,
then loosed in Saturday night halls.

There are songs through crane country, emu foot,
through the blue hymnal's unstitched spine,

through opera vinyl's brylcreem whorl,
Delmae's enfolding lullabye.

3. Earth Cry

Pan's hard hooves churn the riverbank to mud.
        A tick behind his ear poisons the blood
        pumping his haunches' slow paralysis.
Mired to the shins, he wheezewhistles old tunes.
Then his purse ears collect the droning pulse
    of country breathing
    through a wood-bored throat
as if breath were its circulating blood,
the gully were its flute, gorge its bassoon,
        ululations through plateau and rift
        pulling all the stops of the earth's cry,
as if this first cause of tectonics and of song
were root to Adams, jungle, techno, Glass.
        I hear you're quite the dij player; we shall see
        was Sculthorpe's now-you're-pissing
-with-the-big-dogs dig.
Barton's timbred laugh reverberates
    with the good grace of his belief
    in grounds beyond himself, a meeting place
that precedes and makes fluid Concert Hall
arrangement of desk, podium, and pit.
        Now he evokes a tin shed backing onto rail
        -way lines upfurnished with guitar and dij,
his voice bending tradition's flattened notes
in charged magnetic fields. A feral goat
    is grazing in the foyer/in the yard
    scratching his ear. Here is a repertoire
        sufficient to our sky's great gig.

4. Desert Stars Dancing
(with Anthony Garcia)

Desert stars dancing are unsteepled bells
tied off on pegs of acoustic guitars.

They chime when whitewater falls
through black sky raising a nebula

of smoke and dust as desert stars strike
an octave above hum tone fires.

Look up, lying flat, through hours and years
to see stars dance in concentric wheels

and understand sky is the land's dark glass,
twin mirrors charactered with the same dreams.

Dream painters don't need to have flown.
You only look from Economy, down.

Listen: you will hear desert stars toll
through millennia things elders tell.

5. Chant of the Earth

The programme ends as always
with a duet played by guest and host.
Just a few minutes: time enough
to recollect and to inscribe

topographies of spirit and sand
known in the breath and fingertips
onto a mineral seamed sky
where silver, blazing, strikes from lead;

time to bear witness, time enough
for counting out the beats of rain
from signature to drums of storm,
for a road sung to Cammeraygal.

P.S.

Don't let me pass. No, don't let me pass.
Don't call the jarring tumbril an express.
That is no dress rehearsal in the hearse.
We're going nowhere. This is not a test.

Lock up your dictionaries with child-safe locks.
Put them to sleep, your ailing family pets.
Insist on your wrong commas for full-stops.
Banish *la petite mort* from passé sex.

But don't speak in bad faith when I am cold.
Cover your nose and mouth to save your breath.
Pass the time, pass judgement, or pass wind.
But please grant me the dignity of death.

Afterword

Many poems in this volume are shaped by my desire to speak other than in the conventional lyric voice, to enter the region of the discursive essay, for example. While moving beyond the writer's consciousness, experience, and opinion is, ultimately and strictly, impossible, perhaps the privileged sensibility of the poet need not be the declared and unexamined *measure* of things. I hope that the poems' substrata of allusion prompt readers to pursue varied and extended threads of thought, and perhaps to engage anew with the persistence of the past, my most recurrent concern in this book. Engagement with the natural world is also a recurrent theme, music a recurrent motif, so bird noises (and silences) abound.

The five long poems are the bones of the volume, sitting within four parts that evolve in focus and tone, though the divisions are not strict. 'James Martin and James Martin' begins to explore the interactions and disconnections between art and what it takes as its subject matter, on both personal and societal scales, in both contemporary and historical contexts. It takes issue with a Magic-Happens-bumper-sticker faith in art. The second section 'Feral' seeks expanded definitions and tentative recategorizations, inviting the reader to replace with a 'dork descending' Vaughn Williams' ascending lark, to perceive beauty and dignity in the butcher's work, to hold in mind Da Vinci and the Rolling Stones, John Donne and the Red Hot Chili Peppers, and to rethink a too-neat binary of native and feral. 'Rain' gives voice to fears and dissatisfactions, while 'Duet' consciously moves from the iconoclasm of some of the earlier poems towards reconciliations and qualified hopes. The Red Square in which Jack Mundey finds himself is situated, counter to our expectations, in leafy, affluent Hunters Hill.

Formal control matters to me, and increasingly my experience is that a particular poem dictates to me a preferred form and style—be it free verse, terza rima, or sonnet—its line length, its diction. It seems ridiculous to me to believe in a hierarchy of poetries.

Notes

'The Incinerator Art Space': The poem references pen and ink drawings by Drew Truslove exhibited in the Incinerator Art Space, Willoughby, in February 2024.

'Dodge the Dodo' is the title of a 1999 track by the Esbjorn Svensson Trio.

'Flea,' a.k.a. Michael Balzary, is bassist of Red Hot Chili Peppers. The poem, riffing off John Donne's 'The Flea,' is written in admiration for the 60-year-old's gymnastic antics at Sydney Olympic stadium on 4 February 2023.

'Feral' germinated in my reading of Tim Low's *Feral Future: The Untold Story of Australia's Exotic Invaders* (Penguin, 1999). The phrase 'the new nature' is Low's, as is the definition of Botanic Gardens as 'zoos for plants.' Any scientific errors in the poem are my own.

'Nothing to Declare' includes a line, slightly altered, from Ted Hughes' 'Hawk Roosting'.

'Rain': the quotation from Kitty Flanagan is from *Thoughts on Jazz Music*, youtube posted 17 June 2020. Part 6 reworks a line from Bob Dylan's 'A Hard Rain's a-Gonna Fall' (1963).

'Imagine': John Lennon and Yoko Ono met when he visited her show at Soho's Indica Gallery on November 7, 1966. He has said that had the word been 'no' he would not have been moved by her art. 'Hello, Good-Bye' and 'The Fool on the Hill' were both released in 1967.

'Sightings' is in dialogue with Kenneth Slessor's 'Five Visions of Captain Cook' (1931), interrogating, through an analogous subject, Slessor's assumptions about exploration, heroism and history. My poem offers no vision of Matthew Flinders, only a few exploratory sightings of the man, and of shifting coastlines. References are to

Ernest Scott, *The Life of Matthew Flinders* (1914): Matthew Flinders, *The Voyage to Terra Australis* (1814), edited and introduced by Tim Flannery (2000); Jaya Savige, 'Exchange at Skirmish Point' (2005). Readers of Slessor will recognise my reworking of his conceit of the two ship's clocks. The epigraph is from Edward Said, *Orientalism* (1978), Penguin Classics edition 2019, page 50.

'Easter Weekend, Saint Kilda': The poem's conclusion reworks images from the opening line and chorus of Paul Kelly's song 'From Saint Kilda to Kings Cross' (1985).

'Duet': The ABC Classic *Duet* programme aired on 11 November 2021 featured William Barton in conversation with Tamara Anna Cislowska. The five section titles of the poem are titles of items from the programme's playlist on that day. I have at two points transcribed (in italics), and elsewhere drawn on, William Barton's remarks in that broadcast.

Acknowledgements

Thank you to the editors of the following publications, and judges of prizes, in which some of these poems first appeared or achieved some success:

'Whaling' was a finalist in the Montreal International Poetry Prize 2024 (publication forthcoming); 'Inheritance' was a finalist in the Australian Catholic University Prize for Poetry and published in the anthology *Faith* (2024); 'Feral' was a finalist in the Newcastle Poetry Prize and published in the anthology *Measures of Truth* (2020); 'Trip Advisor' was long-listed for the Peter Porter Poetry Prize (2023); 'Sunflowers' was published in *Rabbit* 35 (2022); 'Open the Frog App' was published in *Cordite* 106 (2022), 'Dodge the Dodo' in *Cordite* 105 (2022), and 'Easter Weekend, Saint Kilda' in *Cordite* 114 (2024); 'RUOK?' and 'Imagine' were published in *Shot Glass Journal* 43 (2024).

Thank you to David Dyer, Jamie Grant, Luke Harley, and Alexa Moses for their interest in my work. Thanks especially to Alex Skovron for his fellowship and generous feedback, and for the inspiration of his volume *Letters from the Periphery* (Puncher and Wattmann, 2021), my favourite Australian collection of recent years. Thank you to Drew Truslove for permission to use his *Minnamurra River—Courage Tree—initial sketch* as cover image. Thank you to Shane Strange for bringing the manuscript to publication. And thanks again to Sarah, Anna, and Beth for the love and support without which nothing would be achieved.

About the Author

James Lucas was born in Sydney in 1965. He was educated at the University of New South Wales, where he won the University medal, and then Cambridge, where he completed a Ph D in modernist poetry in 1997. Since his first poetry publication in *Southerly* in 1994, his poems have appeared in *Communion, Contrapasso, Cordite Poetry Review, Heat, Island, Meanjin, New England Review, Overland, Quadrant, Rabbit, Salt, Scarp, Southerly, The Shot Glass*, and in the Henry Kendall Award, Newcastle Poetry Prize, and Australian Catholic University Prize anthologies. His previous volume *Rare Bird* was short-listed for the Anne Elder Award. For many years he has taught English at Sydney Grammar School. He is dismayed by the current vogue for Wallace Stevens.

www.ingramcontent.com/pod-product-compliance
Lightning Source LLC
Chambersburg PA
CBHW020544080526
44583CB00013B/985